ANCIENT CHINA

天子萬年

ANCIENT CHINA

by Michael Gibson

Illustrated by John Berry

GRANADA
London Toronto Sydney New York

Granada Publishing Limited
Frogmore, St Albans, Herts AL2 2NF
and
36 Golden Square, London W1R 4AH
866 United Nations Plaza, New York, NY 10017, USA
117 York Street, Sydney, NSW 2000, Australia
100 Skyway Avenue, Rexdale, Ontario, M9W 3A6, Canada
61 Beach Road, Auckland, New Zealand

Published by Granada Publishing 1982

British Library Cataloguing in Publication Data

Gibson, Michael
Ancient China. – (Granada guide series; 17)
1. China – History – To 1766 B.C. – Juvenile literature
2. China – History – 1766 B.C.–220 A.D. – Juvenile literature
I. Title
931 DS741.5

ISBN 0 246 11799 0

Designed and edited by Holland & Clark Ltd.
Printed and bound in Great Britain by
William Collins Sons & Co Ltd, Glasgow

Contents

The Chinese People	6
Warlords and Emperors	8
Rich and Poor	20
An Empire at Work	30
The Arts	42
Religion	50
Index	62

The Chinese People

On the opposite side of the world to Europe lies the vast land of China. It extends over 3000 kilometres from east to west and from north to south. Its climate varies from sub-arctic to sub-tropical. In the east it faces the Yellow Sea while high mountains dominate the west. In between lie a series of river valleys.

A quarter of the world's people live in this land, which is forty times larger than Britain. Because few western people in our times have visited China, much about the Chinese seems strange to us. Their language seems complicated and they have completely different ways of reading and writing.

Remains of Old Stone Age Man dating from about half a million years ago have been discovered in many parts of China. These people were hunters, fishers and gatherers of berries and nuts. In about 3000 BC Neolithic men introduced farming and stock breeding to China. They settled in the North China Plain which was covered in rich soil. This, watered by the mighty Yellow River, proved to be ideal farming land.

Around 2000 BC, civilized people came to China from the west. According to legend, a chieftain called the Yellow Emperor, Huang Ti, made himself their master. Members of one powerful dynasty (family) called the Hsia were said to have ruled until 1500 BC. As yet, archaeologists have failed to discover any actual evidence of these people. They have discovered much, however, about the Shang who ruled after them. With them the true history of China begins – a civilization that was to last without a break for three and a half thousand years.

This map of China shows the site of the Shang towns and the course of the Yellow River. The earliest civilization in Chinese history grew up in the Yellow River valley with its rich soils and plentiful water supply. When the river flooded, it deposited rich soil over the surrounding countryside, but the floods also needed to be controlled. It was partly for reasons of flood control that a strong central government grew up.

Warlords and Emperors

According to legend, Chinese civilization began in 2205 BC, but for many years there was no evidence to support this claim. Then, in the 1930s, archaeologists discovered an ancient city called Anyang. As a result they learnt a great deal about a civilized people called the Shang who lived in about 1300 BC. They were farmers who dug the soil with hoes and mattocks and irrigated the fields. They grew millet, rice and wheat, built splendid chariots, made cloth out of silk and flax and made weapons, vessels and works of art from bronze.

Shang society was divided into two classes – warrior lords and peasants. Peasants owed allegiance to

A Shang warrior drives a chariot. The Shang was the earliest civilization of which evidence has been discovered in China.

their lord who in turn owed allegiance to the king.

The Shang built many towns, with streets and blocks of houses carefully planned. The peasants lived in crude pit dwellings; the nobles and kings in splendid palaces.

The Shang sacrificed both men and animals to their gods. When their kings died, their tombs were filled with everyday things and luxury articles for use in the next world. Archaeologists have recovered large numbers of bronze, jade, pottery and stone articles as well as the skeletons of hundreds of slaves and charioteers who were buried alive with the dead king.

The Shang knew how to read and write, and made books out of bamboo strips. The language they wrote was similar to modern Chinese. It is probable that it was invented by priests trying to foretell the future.

The Warring States

In about 1100 BC, the Shang were overthrown by a primitive, warlike people from western China called the Chou. The Chou kings gave their friends and relatives great estates to govern in an effort to rule their land effectively. The system did not work, however, for these people rose in revolt and tried to make themselves independent. The only way that the Chou could keep control was by having bigger and stronger armies than their nobles.

In order to teach their subjects respect, they insisted on them *kowtowing*. The nobles had to kneel down before them three times in succession and knock their heads on the floor three times.

Every year the nobles had to give the king presents or tribute in the form of grain and jade in return for their estates. When the king passed through their

Under the Chou, there were long periods of almost continuous warfare when China was divided into many states.

lands, they had to go to his court and kowtow. In this way he constantly reminded them who was in charge.

In order to keep their troublesome lords occupied, the Chou kings fought many wars and conquered all the land around the Yangtze River. This policy worked quite well until it was discovered how to make iron weapons. Then, the nobles were able to ensure that their soldiers were as well armed as the king's. Gradually, the most powerful nobles made themselves independent. Worse still, these great nobles started to fight among themselves and China became one vast battlefield. The ordinary people were miserable, and for a time it seemed that Chinese civilization would be destroyed. To add to the chaos, northern China was invaded by nomadic peoples at this period.

The First Emperor

After two hundred years of bitter civil war, the lord of the state of Chin conquered the other states, and the Chin empire was formed. The Chin emperors broke the power of the great lords and ruled their country through civil servants. The empire was divided into provinces, ruled by governors.

The greatest of the Chin rulers was Chin Shih Huang Ti, who ruled between 221 and 210 BC. His mighty armies conquered the whole of China. He simplified the Chinese language and made everybody in his empire use it. Weights and measures were standardized and coins minted. A network of roads and canals was constructed that linked the capital with every part of the empire.

The first Emperor Chin Shih Huang Ti (left). According to an ancient Chinese historian, he was 'a man with a big nose, large eyes, the chest of a bird of prey and the face of a jackal. He was without kindness and had the heart of a tiger or a wolf'.

The first emperor paid particular attention to communications. The Yellow, Yangtze and West rivers provided good east-west trade routes. Canals were built (right) connecting the great rivers. He had the so-called Magic Canal cut joining the Yangtze and West rivers. This helped him to conquer south China.

The Emperor encouraged the reclamation of farmland from the marshes, and gave the farmers control of their land. Although he did not like merchants, trade flourished during his reign. He hated the scholars who were always quarrelling among themselves. He feared that they would cause civil wars and killed them without mercy – 460 were buried alive on his orders.

During this first emperor's reign, hundreds of thousands of people were set to work building palaces. Archaeologists have uncovered an enormous palace at Hsienyang, the capital. According to legend, this palace was filled with thousands of concubines (secondary wives) captured from other princes. Chinese historians claim that he was the greatest and most frightening man to rule China.

The Great Wall

On countless occasions during her history, China has been invaded by hordes of Mongols from the Great Steppes of Asia. These stocky nomadic people wandered from place to place with their flocks and herds. They rode tough little ponies and were ferocious fighters.

Because of their continuous attacks, the Chinese emperors were forced to maintain tens of thousands of soldiers in the northern provinces. Over the years, castles and stretches of wall were built in some provinces, but there were still plenty of gaps through which the nomads could pour.

When the Emperor Chin Shih Huang Ti came to the throne in 221 BC, he sent his best general, Meng Tien, north with 300,000 soldiers to drive out the invaders and build a continuous wall right across the northern provinces. Meng Tien set to work with a will. His soldiers and the local peasants slaved away up in the mountains and down in the ravines building the Great Wall of China.

The wall was made of pounded earth covered with a layer of bricks and stones. It was between five and ten metres high and about seven metres wide. Beacon towers and blockhouses for sentries were provided at intervals. The wall stretched for 6000 kilometres across some of the most difficult country in China.

Since those days, it has been extended, knocked down and repaired many times. Nevertheless, it remains one of the wonders of the world.

Large numbers of labourers, including many criminals, were used in the construction of the Great Wall.

The First Peasant Revolt

On his death in 210 BC, Chin Shih Huang Ti was the most hated man in China. Hundreds of thousands of peasants had been forced to join the army to defend the frontiers or to build the imperial roads and fortresses. His rule was so brutal and his taxes so high that thousands of peasants fled to the mountains and forests where they lived as outlaws.

After Huang Ti's death, a group of 900 recruits rose in revolt under Chen Sheng and Wu Kuang. Thousands of unhappy peasants joined them. Chen Sheng was elected king. At first all went well as more and more peasants joined the rebels and the imperial armies retreated. But after a few months the peasants were defeated and it seemed that the rebellion was over.

The peasants found two more leaders, Liu Pang and Hsiang Yu. Liu Pang captured the capital Hsienyang and ended the Chin dynasty, fifteen years after it had started. With the cruel Chin out of the way, Liu Pang and Hsiang Yu quarrelled and fought for the throne. Although Hsiang Yu won battle after battle, Liu Pang was the more popular. Gradually, Hsiang Yu's army melted away and finally he committed suicide in despair. In 202 BC, Liu Pang became Emperor (during his reign he took the name Kao Tsu). He was the first of the Han emperors who were to rule China until AD 24. He restored peace, lowered the taxes and reduced the amount of forced labour, and China prospered once more.

The Chin Emperors created great resentment by forcing vast numbers of peasants into the army. The peasants rose in revolt and in the end destroyed the dynasty.

The Han

The Han dynasty lasted 400 years. The Han emperors – sons of Heaven – were all powerful, but had little to do with the everyday government of the empire which was in the hands of provincial governors and officials.

Agriculture flourished, many canals were dug, and new land was brought into cultivation. Trade was so successful that the Emperor Wu Ti (141–87 BC) nationalized the salt, iron and transport industries. The price of grain was controlled; the government stored it when it was plentiful and released it when it was scarce. All these measures helped to fill the treasury. Wu Ti also placed the minting of coins under state control.

A Han Emperor is shown here receiving petitioners. Although the Han were more merciful than the Chin, their nobles were still disloyal. At first the emperors insisted that they live at their capital. After a time, this rule became impossible to enforce. Then the Han weakened the nobles' power by making them divide their land among their sons.

Rich and Poor

A typical Chinese family was much larger then ours. When sons grew up and married, they and their wives lived in their parents' houses. Grandparents were always treated with the greatest respect and, when they became ill or too old to work, they were looked after by the rest of the family. The family played an important part in the development of Chinese society. For example, the idea of government grew out of it. The father was the head of the family and his children obeyed him without question. In the same way the emperor was the father of his people and expected them to obey him instantly.

Women were expected to do exactly what their fathers or husbands told them. When a wealthy

A rich man is carried through lines of humble workers. It was easy to tell peoples' social positions in Ancient China from the clothes they wore. The poor wore simple clothes made out of coarse cloth. But the rich were able to deck themselves out in highly coloured and beautifully decorated silk gowns and robes.

woman got married, she took her servants or some female relatives with her to her new home. These women often became her husband's concubines. Quite often wives and concubines quarrelled, particularly over their children.

The Chinese looked upon children as their hope for the future. Babies were carefully looked after. They were kept in cradles or carried on their mother's back in a fold in her dress. As soon as they could walk, they were dressed in miniature adult clothes. Boys played with hoops, kites and toy soldiers and little girls with dolls, dolls' houses and toy cooking sets. At about the age of six, boys and girls were separated. The sons of well-to-do parents were sent to school where discipline was hard and they were often beaten.

Clothes and Jewellery

In Ancient China you could tell whether a person was rich or poor and from which class he came by studying his clothes. During the winter labourers wore large baggy trousers, tied with tape at the ankles and waist. Their fur-lined coats were made of coarse hemp. In summer they wore long, loose cotton shirts with flapping tails tucked into their belts to form roomy pockets.

Rich men wore the same kind of clothes all the year round: full length garments rather like modern dressing gowns, with long flowing sleeves into which they tucked their hands in cold weather. A belt or wide silk sash was worn around the waist. In Imperial times hats were very important, as each grade

Chinese women powdered their faces with pollen dust, rubbed patches of rouge on their lips and cheeks, and painted their eyelids blue-green. They had their hair dressed in elaborate styles and decorated with jewellery.

These Chinese peasants are going to work. They are carrying a spear, a scythe, a flail, a hammer and a mattock.

of official had a different kind which could be easily recognised. Sometimes, they wore turbans made out of long strips of silk.

Peasant women wore long woollen gowns in winter and cotton dresses in summer. Wealthy women, however, had dresses made of silk. The upper dress was richly embroidered and cut low so that the under dress of a different colour could be seen. Jewelled belts or girdles circled the waist. Jade necklaces and brooches completed the outfit. Hair was brushed into elaborate shapes and held in place with metal or bone pins and fancy combs. Faces were powdered and cheeks and eyelids painted.

Feasting and Food

Chinese peasants were always close to starvation. Their food was simple and small in quantity.

Throughout its history, China has had a teeming population, and food shortages and famines have been a constant problem. The peasants have nearly always been close to starvation. The most they could expect was two meagre meals a day. In the north, their diet consisted of cakes of millet or soya bean flour, meat dumplings, eggs and occasionally a chicken. The Chinese disliked most dairy products so their meals lacked milk, butter and cheese.

In the south the main food was rice, sometimes mixed with bamboo shoots. All cooking was done in metal or earthenware pots. The food was served in pottery bowls and eaten with chopsticks instead of knives and forks. Tea was the normal drink in the south. (It was not drunk in the north until much later.) Boiling water was poured over a few dried

The rich attended banquets where they ate many types of food and enjoyed all kinds of entertainment.

leaves in a bowl and the steaming liquid served in smaller handleless bowls.

The rich could afford much more exciting food, including melons, pears, lichees, mangoes and grapes. Certain famous Chinese delicacies, such as bird's nest soup, originated in ancient times. Important occasions were celebrated with feasts. These splendid meals took up to half a day to eat. The guests were seated according to their rank. Dishes of food were handed around by young girls and the guests helped themselves to whatever they wanted. In between courses, bowls of scented water and silken napkins were carried round so that the guests could wash and dry their hands. Even though there was so much variety, the Chinese were never greedy and only ate a little from each course.

At Home

In Ancient China the houses of the ordinary people were usually great sprawling affairs made of mud bricks. The roofs were thatched with straw in which all manner of bugs, animals and birds made their homes. The floor was lower than the ground outside and there was a fireplace in a central sunken pit. In the south many people lived in simple bamboo huts.

Town houses owned by well-to-do people were more elaborate. They were built of wood and brick and had tiled roofs. The rooms were usually built around a central courtyard. These houses were often several storeys high. Pictures of the gods were painted on the front doors to frighten away demons. As a second line of defence, there were screens just inside the door that evil spirits could not squeeze past. As the Chinese believed that evil spirits always moved in straight lines, they made their roofs dip and slope at every opportunity.

By modern standards, both kinds of houses had little furniture. The Chinese believed in simplicity. A living room usually contained only a long, low wooden table surrounded by cushions instead of chairs. The only other furniture would be a cupboard or chest in which the family valuables were stored. The family slept in little bare rooms containing simple straw mattresses.

The furniture of the rich was much the same as that of the poor, though their rooms would contain more cupboards and chests, richly decorated and covered in shiny lacquer. Instead of bedrolls laid directly on the floor, they had proper beds covered with silk quilts. Their rooms were beautifully painted and decorated.

This illustration shows what a rich man's house was like in Han times. Many models of this kind of house have been found in Han tombs. The Chinese believed that evil spirits always moved in straight lines. To keep them away, they introduced all kinds of slopes and dips into their buildings, including the turned-up eaves that are so characteristic of the buildings of Ancient China.

Sport and Entertainment

Among the Ancient Chinese of all classes, games and sports were particularly popular. The rich, for example, had a passion for hunting. They tracked down and killed almost every kind of creature that ran, swam or flew. They loved to hunt antelope, deer, wild boar, bears and even tigers. Specially bred hounds were used to raise, track and kill game. Wild duck, geese and other water fowl were shot with bows and arrows.

Gambling was another obsession. A game called Liu-po was extremely popular. Six bamboo sticks were shaken out of a holder like dice and the players moved counters about a board according to their score. Contemporary pictures show players in a high state of excitement.

Both rich and poor enjoyed a great variety of entertainment. There were dancers, jugglers, acrobats, story tellers and skilful musicians to be found in both towns and villages. The best entertainers appeared in the imperial palaces and the homes of the rich. Less successful performers worked in market places and village inns. Cock fighting and dog and horse racing were also popular. In addition, there were many trials of skill and strength including wrestling and weight lifting. Models of athletes and games players are often found in Han tombs.

In Ancient China travelling players provided much of the entertainment. Jugglers, wrestlers and knife throwers appeared at markets and festivals.

An Empire at Work

Agriculture was the mainstay of Chinese civilization. Farming began in the Yellow and Yangtze river valleys in about 3500 BC when New Stone Age men started to grow millet. Gradually, they learnt how to domesticate dogs and pigs and later sheep, cattle, horses and chickens. The next advance came with the invention of the ox-drawn plough in Chou times. This greatly improved food production as ploughs cut much deeper into the soil than spades. The Chou grew wheat, maize, rice, sorghum and beans, although hunting remained an important source of food.

Although the peasants grew the food that fed the whole population, they themselves were never far from starvation. During prosperous periods the population increased rapidly. But although there were many more mouths to feed, there was only the same amount of good farming land to grow food on. The Chinese therefore had to cultivate every possible centimetre of ground. The sides of the hills were terraced. The plains were irrigated with water drawn from the rivers and distributed through the fields by means of canals and ditches. Where rivers tended to overflow their banks, huge mounds of earth were piled up to hold back the water. As a result the land of China looked like a patchwork quilt of many-coloured fields. Here and there, shining silver streams and rivers flowed through them providing life-giving water.

As long as the peasants were healthy, China was successful. They were the country's greatest strength. If they sickened, so did the state.

The Chinese were expert farmers and made use of every square centimetre of ground. The hillsides were terraced and the plains were well irrigated.

Industry

Although farming was the foundation of China's success, other industries gradually developed. The Emperor and his nobles loved luxuries and set up workshops and factories to manufacture them. Imperial agencies employed expert metalworkers, carpenters, painters and textile workers.

By about 100 BC, the emperors had also become interested in mining. They noticed that some of their subjects were making huge fortunes from mining iron and salt so they nationalized these industries and took the profits for themselves.

The Chinese also made effective use of water power. From about AD 100, water wheels were used to raise water on to the fields to grind corn and to work the bellows for blast furnaces.

The Chinese made considerable use of water power. This tilt hammer was driven by a water wheel.

An imperial workshop. The Chinese emperors took over a number of industries and collected the profits.

By the Han period, there were true industrial towns in the province of Honan, where the people worked in mines and foundries. These craftsmen produced ploughs, spades and hoes, as well as iron and bronze swords, spear and arrow heads, armour and helmets.

Along the coast of the Shantung peninsula, salt was produced by diverting the sea into shallow pans where the water evaporated, leaving the salt behind. Elsewhere, in Manchuria, the Ordos desert and Ssu-ch'uan, salt had to be mined. Some of the pits went down as deep as 600 metres. As well as considerable skill, the engineers used drills to dig the mine shafts and winding gear and pulleys to lift and lower buckets. By the time of Christ there were no less than 34 imperial agencies producing salt.

The Silk Industry

The Chinese silk industry is very ancient, though historians do not know exactly when it started. It was certainly well established by Shang times. By the Han period, the Chinese were supreme in silk manufacture and their products were imported by the Romans.

We know almost nothing about how the earliest Chinese made silk cloth, as none of their tools or machines have survived to the present day. However, fragments of silk have been found which were made in very early times. It is likely that silk clothes were so expensive that they were worn until they literally fell to pieces.

Workers collect mulberry leaves on which the silk 'worms', or larvae, feed.

Silk worms feed on mulberry leaves in specially prepared trays. Later the worms surround themselves with a covering, or cocoon, made of hundreds of metres of silk thread.

Silk moths lay their eggs on mulberry leaves. After eight to ten days the silk worms (caterpillars) hatch out and spend the next four weeks crunching their way through piles of mulberry leaves. Then the worms start to spin cocoons. Each caterpillar produces a continuous thread about 900 metres long. Normally, when the adult insect emerges from its cocoon the silk is damaged, so the Chinese killed the pupae by heating them. The silk thread was then reeled, and woven on horizontal looms with the long warp threads spread along the whole length.

Accounts written in Han times describe silks of many different colours including dazzling whites, reds, blues, and greens. Even more beautiful cloths contained threads made of gold. Taffetas, gauzes, crepes and damasks were all produced in various designs.

Transport

In a country the size of China, a good transport system was essential. Fortunately, a number of wide, navigable rivers, including the Yellow and the Yangtze Kiang, flow from west to east. As the Chinese towns grew larger their population required considerable quantities of food, which was supplied by river. By the end of the sixth century AD, the lower Yangtze valley provided the capital with all the grain it needed. The transport system was improved by the construction of a string of canals, and a network of excellent roads. Unlike Roman roads, these were only thin, lightweight surfaces resting on the subsoil.

Much of China's produce was carried in ox-carts or waggons drawn by donkeys. In the mountains mules

The Chinese built suberb chariots and bred magnificent trotting horses. Many model chariots have been found in graves.

The invention of the wheelbarrow did a great deal to improve the life of the Chinese peasant.

served as beasts of burden, while camels carried goods across the deserts of the north west. The rich rode in carriages or on horseback. By Han times, fine two-wheeled carriages pulled by trotting horses had been developed. In the second century AD the wheelbarrow was invented and quickly became an important means of transport. At the same time boats like sampans plied up and down the rivers, while larger ships sailed the open seas carrying Chinese goods throughout the Far East.

Large boats, looking much like modern sampans, sailed up and down the Chinese rivers.

Trade

Although Chinese rulers and nobles always regarded trading with deep contempt, it nevertheless formed an important part of China's life. Even the Shang produced surplus goods for sale and accepted cowrie shells in return. Under the Chou, trading prospered to such an extent that metal coins were minted. Later still, the Han are said to have introduced paper money.

Chinese merchants settled in the towns where the goods they sold were manufactured and where markets were held. Shops and stalls were set out in neat rows, each dealing with a particular kind of product.

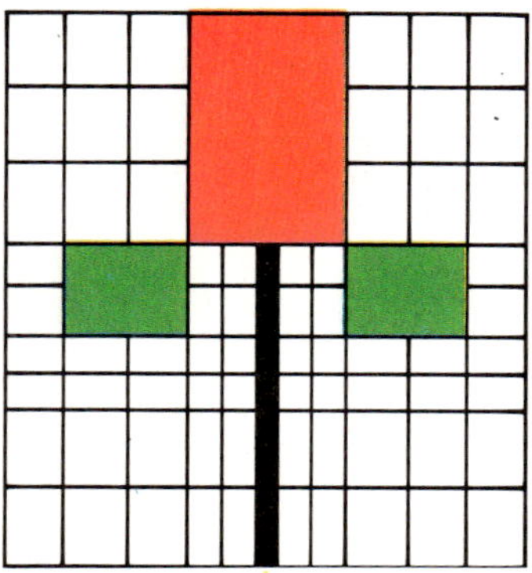

Chinese towns were always built as simple squares (above) with their streets running north-south and east-west. They were protected from attack by walls and moats. They were often important centres of trade.

There were sections for butchers, grocers and many others.

The Ancient Chinese seem to have exported iron, bronze and lacquer wares as well as silk. Jade was imported from Central Asia. Pearls, glass and wild animals including lions and rhinos for the imperial zoo were imported from the south. Slaves were also brought from Europe.

The most important incident in China's trading history was the sending of the first caravan to Western Europe in 106 BC. The opening of this great trade route, known as the Silk Road, was probably the accidental result of the Emperor Wu Ti's search for allies.

Every Chinese town had a market where produce was exchanged or bought and sold.

The Army

Although the Chinese claimed to despise war and soldiers, they made as much of their warriors as any other people. Chinese warriors wore helmets and thick, padded silk coats covered with leather or steel plates, and carried leather shields. The foot-soldiers had no armour. The Han made crossbows out of horn and bone as well as wood, and they were fine archers. They also fought with knives and spears called ko-halberds, which consisted of a blade (ko) mounted on a wooden pole.

A Chinese army was a blaze of colour. Banners floated above it and the armour and weapons glinted in the sun. Battles were fought according to strict rules.

Long before they had cavalry, the Chinese produced fine two-wheeled chariots. The charioteers drove their vehicles into the thick of battle and hurled their spears or fired their arrows into the crowded ranks of footsoldiers.

Battles were colourful affairs. Everywhere, great banners floated on the breeze. They bore pictures of symbolic animals such as the Red Bird of the South, the Black Tortoise of the North, the White Tiger of the West and the Green Dragon of the East. The gaudily-clad warriors, with their shining weapons and armour, hurled taunts at each other before dashing into the fray. For all their armour, they were no safer from arrows and crossbow bolts then the ordinary footsoldiers. Many a noble was cut down and left dead or dying on the battlefield.

The Arts

The earliest examples of Chinese writing have been found on animal shoulder blades used by Shang sorcerers to foretell the future. The bones were first heated; then the magicians studied the way in which they cracked, and wrote down their predictions on the bone. During the Chou period scholars started to write books. The earliest book found so far dates from 841 BC. The characters, or picture words, were painted on to strips of bamboo.

Although no earlier Chinese books have been discovered, we know that they existed because they were copied by generation after generation of scribes and have come down to us in later versions. Most of

All the various processes of book making were carried out in the same workshop. Scribes painted characters on strips of bamboo which were laced together like Venetian blinds.

these early books were chronicles, that is lists of dates and descriptions of the reigns of kings and emperors.

Few people could read in Ancient China. In practice, only the very rich and important had the time and opportunity to learn. However, the Chou kings did open a few schools to educate poor children.

Chinese words are very different from ours. Instead of making up words with letters of the alphabet, a different character or simplified picture is used for each word. By 202 BC there were 3000 of these characters. During the Han period writers and scholars invented another 6000. By the time the first Chinese dictionary had been compiled in AD 121 there were many many more.

Music and Theatre

The Ancient Chinese did not have as many kinds of entertainment as we do today, so the theatre was a great source of amusement. Some plays took three whole days to perform. The actors wore beautiful costumes and moved about in a flowing way rather like modern ballet dancers. All the women's parts were taken by young boys. As there was no scenery, actors carried boards across the stage to tell the audience where the action was supposed to be taking place. Families sat on the floor and ate their meals while the play was still going on. They often knew the words by heart.

Chinese music seems strange to western ears. It is supposed to sound like dripping water, bird song or thunder and lightning. In ancient times no music was written down: musicians learnt tunes off by heart. The Chinese played stringed instruments like mandolines, lutes and zithers, and wind intruments like flutes, whistles, oboes and horns. There were also strange percussion instruments like gongs, cymbals and tambourines, as well as all kinds of drums. In addition the Chinese loved bells. Large bells were struck with a hammer and tiny ones were hung in the trees to be played by the wind.

Gorgeously costumed actors conveyed meaning by exaggerated gestures. Their thick-soled shoes helped the audience to see them better.

Creative Craftsmen

This beautifully decorated leopard was found in the tomb of a Han princess called Tou Wan in 1968.

The Ancient Chinese produced a great variety of beautiful objects. From the earliest days they were experts in bronze work. The Shang made elegant drinking vessels, dishes and bowls. Later, splendid figures of animals were modelled in bronze and decorated with precious stones. The leopards from Tou Wan's tomb are fine examples. The very finest example of this work is the famous flying horse. The horse is shown galloping with only one foot attached to its base. It is a masterpiece of Chinese craftsmanship.

Princess Tou Wan's jade funeral suit (right). She died in the 1st century BC. The suit is made of two thousand pieces of jade knitted together with gold covered wire. Jade was very precious to the Chinese.

This famous 'flying horse' is a masterpiece. Only one foot is joined to the base of the statuette.

At all periods of Chinese history potters were treated with respect. They baked their pots in special kilns, using dry straw and bamboo as fuel. The Shang made red pottery bowls with simple ornaments and drawings. After a time the potters learnt to dip their pots in a fine white slip (paste) which provided a good ground for their stylish paintings. Dishes, tripod bowls and tall beakers were decorated with scenes of everday life or simple picture stories. In later times potters modelled all kinds of figures as well.

Gifted Gardeners

The Chinese have always regarded gardening as an art. Both Taoists and Buddhists encouraged the construction of gardens, which were thought to be essential parts of a house or palace. The gardens were quite different from their European counterparts. They had no neatly mown lawns and beds of flowers; they were miniature landscapes. Their most important elements were rocks and water with flowers, trees and buildings to complete the picture.

Many flowers had particular meanings: for example, the chrysanthemum stood for retirement and culture, the water lily for purity and truth, the bamboo for suppleness and strength. As the Chinese

understood the meaning of each flower, a garden could be read like a book. The weird looking lumps of weather-beaten rock, placed at focal points, helped to remind the householders of the power of nature. So, too, did the streams crossed by elegant wooden bridges. Artificial lakes containing brightly-coloured fish could be admired from the colourful pavilions. The Chinese garden was a miniature world. It was a place where the family could go to think, write or merely find peace and quiet.

A Chinese garden. For the Chinese, gardening was an art. Endless care was put into the creation of a miniature world containing mountains, valleys, rivers, lakes, bridges, paths, trees and plants.

Religion

The Chinese believed that the emperor was chosen by the Heavenly Power. When an emperor was overthrown, it was said to be the will of Heaven. When the first Chou king seized the throne he claimed that the last Shang ruler had been defeated because he was unfit to rule.

The Chinese emperor was a priest as well as a ruler. His people expected him to carry out essential religious ceremonies to ensure China's prosperity. The emperor had to visit holy sites all over his country. Every year, for example, he climbed Mount T'ai in east China and sacrificed bulls to the spirits of Heaven and Earth. The Chinese believed that these ceremonies were necessary if they were to escape floods, droughts and other natural disasters.

From very early times the Chinese worshipped their emperors as gods, and shrines were built to them all over China. Each had to be provided with offerings of food, and with priests and servants to look after the sacred buildings. By Han times the worship of the living and dead god-emperors had become extremely expensive.

Like most people, the Chinese emperors wanted to live for ever. They believed that certain sorcerers could manufacture medicines that would make them immortal. Later, not only the emperors and nobles but even the ordinary people hoped for a life after death.

The emperor was both a god and a high priest. He performed important religious ceremonies, such as this sacrifice, to ensure the prosperity of China.

The Good Life

Confucius, the most famous Chinese teacher of all time, lived from 551 to 479 BC. His Chinese name was K'ung Fu-tzu or Master Kung. Confucius taught that everybody should behave properly. He believed that people could only live happily together if subjects respected their emperor, sons their fathers, younger brothers their elder brothers, wives their husbands and friends each other.

Confucius taught that people should always do what they knew to be right. He used to tell a story about two Shang princes. When their lord was put to death by a Chou king, they refused to become his subjects. Instead, they fled to the mountains and starved themselves to death. Confucius admired their loyalty.

Many disciples joined Confucius and travelled with him around China in search of a good ruler. But no matter where they went they could not find a leader who would follow Confucius's teachings.

Confucius often preached to his followers in the open. His sayings were carefully remembered and written down.

Confucius's words were copied down by his followers and made into a book called the *Analects* (Selected Sayings). For many centuries the first thing Chinese children had to do on entering school was to learn the *Analects* by heart.

Confucius spent much of his time studying accounts of the past. These records were made into books called the *Five Classics*. These too were studied by generation after generation of Chinese scholars. Under the Han Emperor Wu Ti, Confucian teaching became the official state belief.

As the years went by Confucianism became a religion and everybody who wanted to become a civil servant studied the great teacher's works and sat examinations based on them. Only those who achieved the best marks were recognised as scholars and entered the civil service. Confucius taught that the ruling class should be selected on the basis of ability and good conduct – not wealth or status.

The Way of Lao Tzu

While Confucius was trying to persuade the Chinese to live according to his teachings, another group of people called the Taoists were calling for a very different way of life. The word 'Tao' means 'Way'. The Taoists believe that everything in the universe follows a pattern. All that man has to do to be happy is to fit into this pattern. The only way a person can do this is to let life carry him along like a piece of wood in a river. Taoists believe that people should let things take their natural course.

Lao Tzu, the first Taoist, lived at about the same time as Confucius. He is said to have written a book called *The Way and its Power*. It was full of riddles and trick questions designed to make people think. Confucius believed that man was the only thing that mattered. Lao Tzu argued that man was only one of the Ten Thousand Things that made up the Universe, each of which had a purpose of its own. If a man accepted everything that happened to him without question, he would become one with the Way. Such men were recognized as wise men or sages.

The most enthusiastic Taoists became hermits and lived by themselves in the mountains. But this way of life attracted few people. As the years went by, some Taoists believed that they could live for ever with the help of magic drugs and claimed that Lao Tzu had flown up to heaven and was living there with the gods. People started to pray to Lao Tzu and other Taoist sages and soon a new religion had come into being.

Inside this Taoist temple, the faithful worship many gods. Taoists accept life as it is and respect all living creatures. They often believe in magic.

Buddhism

According to legend Ming, a Han Emperor, once dreamed about a huge, gleaming, golden god. On waking, he asked his ministers if they knew who he might be. One of them suggested that he could be the Buddha who was worshipped in India. And so the Emperor sent men to India to find out about him. As a result, Buddhism became China's third great religion.

The Buddha taught that, until people stopped caring for worldly things such as eating, drinking and getting rich, they would have to live life after life. Sometimes they might be reborn as an insect or some other animal, sometimes as another human being. If people gave up their interest in worldly things, however, they would reach Nirvana, a kind of Buddhist heaven.

Although the Taoists liked many Buddhist ideas, the Confucians did not. The Confucians, for instance, believed that having children and keeping the family going was the most important thing in life, but many Buddhists became monks and nuns and had no children. At first, Confucian rulers persecuted the Buddhists and closed down their monasteries.

Gradually, however, the Chinese reshaped Buddhism to suit their own needs. Indeed, they changed it so much that it was difficult to recognize it as the same religion that was practised in India. The Chinese, for example, believed that if they repeated Buddha's name over and over again they would go to a paradise called 'the pure land' when they died.

Rows of faithful Buddhists visit a cave temple containing many stone figures of the Buddha. Buddhists constantly strive for personal salvation.

Festivals

Life was very hard for ordinary people in Ancient China. There were few holidays, so festivals such as New Year were celebrated with vigour. The men spent the first week hunting and fishing while the women relaxed at home with friends. The children played – practising juggling, walking on stilts, challenging others to tugs-of-war or football, and flying brightly coloured kites. On the last evening of the New Year holiday the Festival of Lanterns was held. The dark streets twinkled with little lanterns of horn or shell containing small wax candles. Then through the town came a huge model dragon, lit from inside by lanterns and carried like a pantomine horse.

The dragon was the god of the rivers, whose waters enabled the crops to grow. On the fifth day of the fifth month, the Dragon Boat festival was held. According to legend, the chief minister of a wicked ruler drowned himself because his master would not change his ways. People were so impressed by his act that they commemorated it each year. Gaily decorated dragon boats were paddled into mid-stream and gifts and food thrown on to the water. After that the boats raced each other, watched by great crowds beating gongs and cymbals. At night, lights were placed on the water and there was much feasting.

The Dragon Boat festival was one of the most popular in Ancient China. Races took place between gaily decorated ships, to the delight of the onlookers.

The Buried Army

In the spring of 1974 the workers on the Yen Tsai commune in Shensi province, west China, discovered one of the most important graves ever to be unearthed. Life size pottery figures of nearly 6000 fully-armed soldiers were found lying several metres beneath the surface. In addition, there were hundreds of horses drawing fully equipped chariots. No two men or horses were alike. Each had been modelled from life. Their swords, spears and crossbows were real. They look as alive today as they did 2200 years ago when they were first placed in their colossal grave.

The great army was buried standing in battle formation in a roofed grave measuring 225 by 65 metres. All this was done in honour of the tyrannous Emperor Chin Shih Huang Ti who lies buried in an unopened tomb one kilometre away. At one time a great artificial hill towered over the proud ruler's last resting place, but all that remains now is a small mound covered in pine trees and wild flowers.

This tomb was originally the centre of a great walled area or spirit city containing temples, towers and sacred inscriptions. Beyond this lay an outer city and another enormous set of walls.

According to legend, all the workers who helped to construct the tomb were murdered on its completion. In the future, Chinese archaeologists will be opening the great tyrant's grave and we must wait until then to discover what treasures he tried to take with him to the next world.

This vast tomb contains thousands of full-sized models of soldiers and horses. They were to be the Emperor Chin Shih Huang Ti's heavenly army.

Index

Actors 44
Alphabet 43
Analects 53
Anyang 8
Archaeology 6, 8, 9, 13, 60–1
Army 10, 40–41
Arts 42–3

Babies 21
Battles 11
Blast furnaces 32
Books 9, 42
Britain 6
Bronze 8, 39, 46
Buddha 56
Buddhism 56–7
Buddhists 48, 56–7
Butchers 39

Camels 37
Canal, the Magic 12
Canals 12, 18, 30, 36
Cattle 30
Chariots 8–9, 37, 41
Chen Sheng 16
Chickens 30
Chin emperors 12–13, 19
Chin Shih Huang Ti 12–13, 14, 16, 60–61
Chinese language 6, 12, 42
Chopsticks 24
Chou emperors 10–11, 30, 38, 42, 50, 52
Civil servants 53
Civil war 10–11, 16–17
Climate 6
Cloth 34–5
Clothes 21, 22–3
Concubines 13, 21
Confucius 52–3, 54
Confucians 52–3, 55, 57
Cooking 24–5
Cowrie shells 38
Craftsmen 46–47

Dancing 29
Dogs 30
Domesticated animals 30
Dragons 58–59

Entertainment 29
Evil spirits 26
Examinations 53

Family 20–1
Farming 6, 18, 30
Feasting 25, 59
Festivals 29, 58–9
Five Classics 53
Flax 8
Flowers 48–9
Flying Horse 46–47
Food 24–5
Forced labour 16–17
Foundries 32
Furniture 26

Gambling 28
Games 21, 28–9, 58
Gardens 48–9
Gods 51–61
Government 18, 20
Graves 9, 27, 29, 46–47, 60–61
Great Wall 14–15
Grocers 39

Han emperors 17–19, 29, 35, 38, 40, 43, 50, 56

Honan Province 32
Horses 14, 29, 30, 60
Houses 26–27
Hsia emperors 6
Hsiang Yu 17
Hsienyang 13, 17
Huang-Ti 6
Hunting 6

India 56–57
Industry 32–33, 34–35
Iron 32, 39
Irrigation 30, 32

Jade 9, 10, 23, 39
Jewellery 22–23

Kao-Tsu 17
Kowtowing 10–11

Lacquer 26, 39
Land reclamation 13
Lanterns 59
Lao Tzŭ 54–55
Legend 6, 8, 13
Liu Pang 17
Liu Po 28
Looms 35

Magic 54
Maize 30
Make-up 22–3
Manchuria 33
Markets 29, 38
Marriage 21
Medicines 50, 54
Merchants 13, 38–39
Millet 8
Ming 56
Mining 33
Minting coins 12, 38
Monasteries 57
Mongols 14
Mulberry leaves 34–35
Music 44–45, 59

Nationalized industries, 18, 32–33
Neolithic times 6, 30
New Stone Age 6, 30
New Year Festival 58–59
Nobles 8–9, 11, 18

Old Stone Age 6
Ordos Desert 33

Palaces 9
Pearls 39
Pigs 30
Plays 44–45
Ploughs 30, 32
Poor people 8–9, 14, 16–17, 22–28, 42
Pottery 9, 24, 46–7, 60
Priests 50, 57

Reading 9, 42
Reclamation of land 13
Religion 50–61
Rice 8, 30
Rich people 22–23, 25, 27, 28, 42
Roads 12, 36–7
Romans 34, 36

Sacrifices 9, 50
Salt 32–33
Scholars 53
Schools 21, 42, 53
Servants 50
Shang emperors 6–7, 8–9, 10, 34, 38, 46, 50, 52
Shantung Province 33
Sheep, 30

Shensi Province 60
Ships 37, 59
Shops 38
Silk 8, 22–23, 34–35, 39
Silk Road 39
Silk worm 35
Slaves 39
Sorcery 42, 50
Songhum, 30
Soya beans 30
Sports 28–29, 58
Ssu-ch'uan salt mines 33
Steppes 14

Taoism 54–55
Taoists 48, 54–55, 57
Taxes 17, 18
Tea 24
Temples 54, 56–57
Terracing 30
Theatre 44–45
Tools 23
Tou Wan, Princess 46
Towns 9, 26, 29, 36
Toys 21
Trade 13, 38–39
Transport 36–37

War 10–11, 16–17
Water power 32
Way and its Power 54
Weapons 32, 40–41, 60–61
Weights and measures 12
West River 12
Wheat 8
Wheel barrows 37
Wives 20–21
Writing 9, 42–43
Wu Kuang 16
Wu-Ti 18, 39, 53

Yangtze Kiang 11, 12, 30, 36
Yellow Emperor 6
Yellow River 7, 12, 30, 36
Yellow Sea 6

Zoo, Imperial 39